CLAY QUESTS
HIDDEN PICTURE PUZZLES

Helena Bogosian

STERLING

New York / London
www.sterlingpublishing.com/kids

STERLING and the distinctive Sterling logo are registered trademarks of
Sterling Publishing Co., Inc.

10 9 8 7 6 5 4 3 2 1

Published by Sterling Publishing Co., Inc.
387 Park Avenue South, New York, NY 10016
© 2008 by Helena Bogosian
Distributed in Canada by Sterling Publishing
c/o Canadian Manda Group, 165 Dufferin Street
Toronto, Ontario, Canada M6K 3H6
Distributed in the United Kingdom by GMC Distribution Services
Castle Place, 166 High Street, Lewes, East Sussex, England BN7 1XU
Distributed in Australia by Capricorn Link (Australia) Pty. Ltd.
P.O. Box 704, Windsor, NSW 2756, Australia

Printed in China

Sterling ISBN 978-1-4027-4754-0

For information about custom editions, special sales, premium and
corporate purchases, please contact Sterling Special Sales
Department at 800-805-5489 or specialsales@sterlingpublishing.com.

CONTENTS

ALIEN OLYMPICS

Each contestant has a matching fan in the stands.
Can you spot all four?

Answer on page 29.

RECYCLE!
These volunteers are collecting cans.
Can you find a match for the four cans on the wall?

Answer on page 30.

PIZZA WITH EVERYTHING

This pizza really has the works.
Can you spot the 12 items that don't belong?

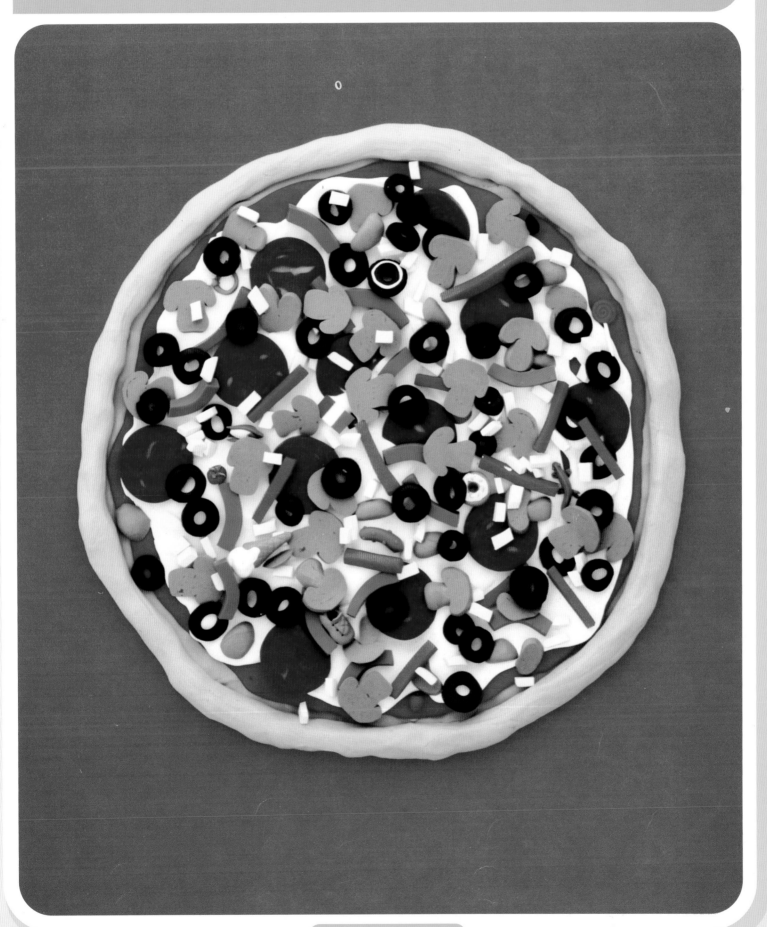

Answer on page 31.

DIRTY LAUNDRY

The socks on the left are missing their pairs.
Can you find them?

Answer on page 32.

COOKIES PLEASE

A customer would like one more of each cookie in the box.
Can you find all of them?

Answer on page 33.

DIG IN

The archeologists are looking for another set of dinosaur bones like those below the rope. Do you see them?

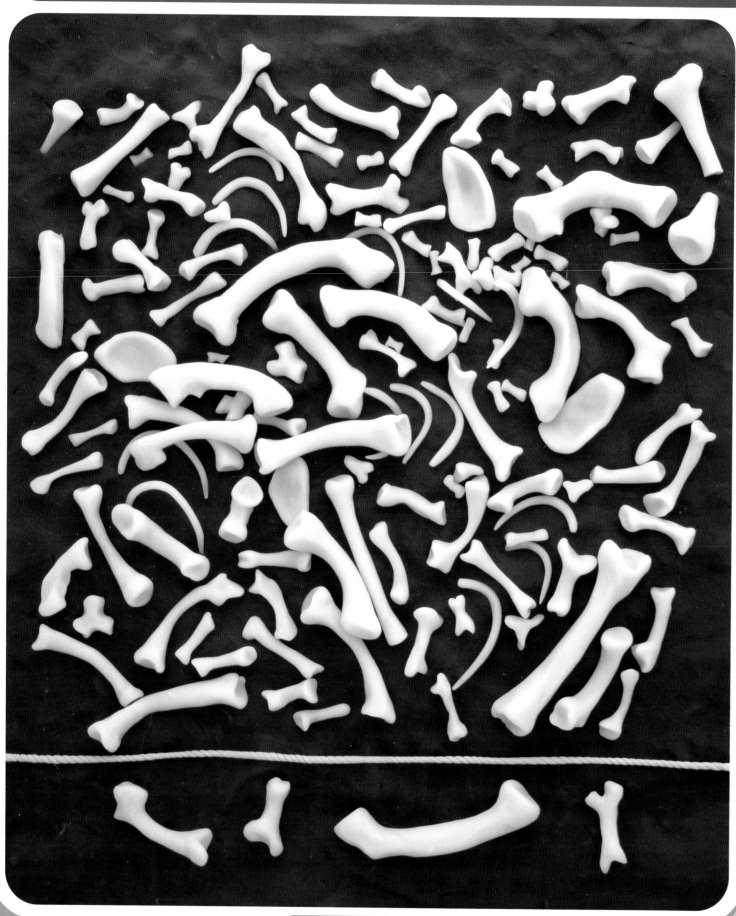

Answer on page 34.

SEW IT UP
These quilts contain the same squares sewn together in a different order.
Can you find the match for each square?

Answer on page 35.

SEEING SPOTS

There are some unique markings on these cows.
Can you locate all nine strange spots?

Answer on page 36.

CRAYON CRAZE

There are four items in this box that you cannot color with.
Do you see them?

Answer on page 37.

DAYCARE EGGS

These nervous egg-sitters need to find the matching siblings for the eggs they are holding. Hurry, before the momma birds come to pick up their kids.

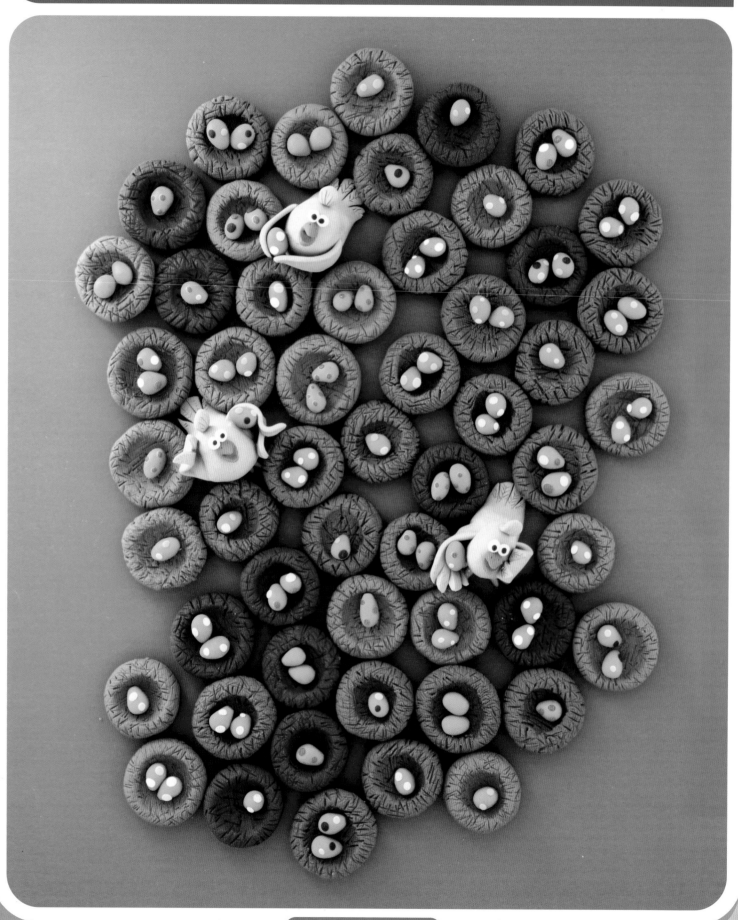

Answer on page 38.

BACKPACK BLAST

What an after school mess! Can you find 13 pencils, four pens, four balls, a pretzel, and a half-eaten sandwich?

Answer on page 39.

FALLING LEAVES

There are a few surprises hiding among the autumn leaves.
Do you see all seven?

Answer on page 40.

WITCH'S LIBRARY

The witch needs help to set the frog-prince free. The answer lies in books of 3. The first is blue with a moon and dot, the second green with black and white spots, and the last is blue with a little black moon.

Answer on page 29.

SECRET RECIPE

The chef is looking for a few items. Help him find the marshmallow, the garlic, the onion, the orange, and the banana.

Answer on page 30.

SHOELACE RACE

Each pair of shoes has only one lace.
Find the missing laces as fast as you can!

Answer on page 31.

PIRATE'S TREASURE

What a discovery! Can you find four rings, two crowns, two goblets, a bracelet, a pair of candlesticks, a pitcher, a bowl, and four spoons?

Answer on page 32.

PICNIC PESTS

These uninvited insects prefer sweet watermelon to sour pickles.
Can you spot all 13 ants?

Answer on page 33.

HIEROGLYPHICS

Not all of these carvings are from Ancient Egypt.
Do you see the 14 that don't belong?

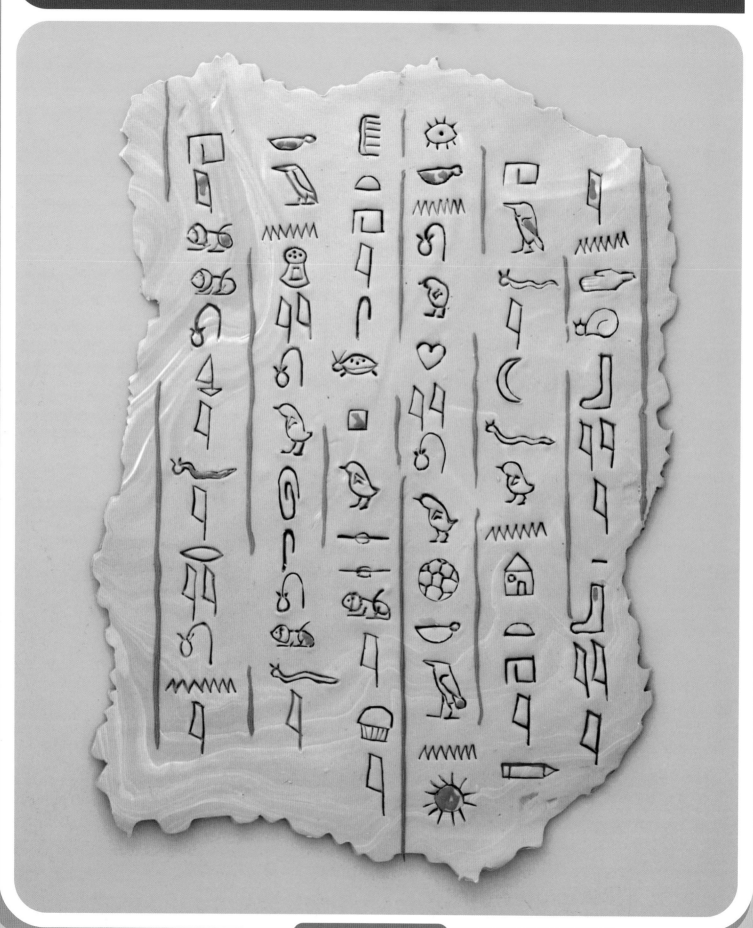

Answer on page 34.

BUTTON HUNT

Some buttons are missing from these garments.
Sort through this pile of buttons to find the perfect match for each jacket.

Answer on page 35.

COLOR CHANGE

There are 12 chameleons using color-changing camouflage to hide.
Can you find them all?

Answer on page 36.

BREAKFAST SPECIAL

One order for today's breakfast special is on the tray.
Can you find the other?

Answer on page 37.

PARLOR GUESTS

Twenty-three tiny guests have come for tea.
How many can you ...

Answer on page 38.

BALLOON FESTIVAL

Help guide the balloons in for a safe landing near the flags.
The pattern on the flag matches the pattern on the balloon.

NEEDLES IN A HAYSTACK

Finding one needle in a haystack is a challenge.
Can you find all 19?

Answer on page 40.

ANSWERS

ALIEN OLYMPICS

WITCH'S LIBRARY

RECYCLE!

SECRET RECIPE

PIZZA WITH EVERYTHING

SHOELACE RACE

DIRTY LAUNDRY

PIRATE'S TREASURE

COOKIES PLEASE

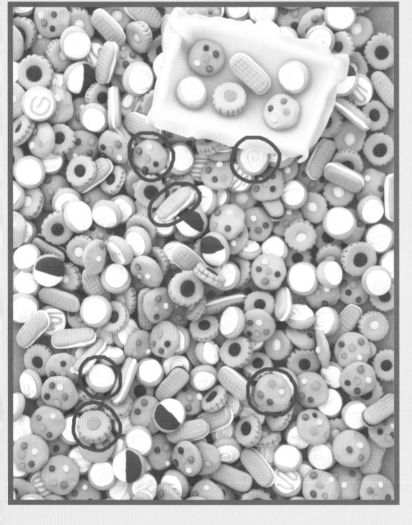

PICNIC PESTS

DIG IN

HIEROGLYPHICS

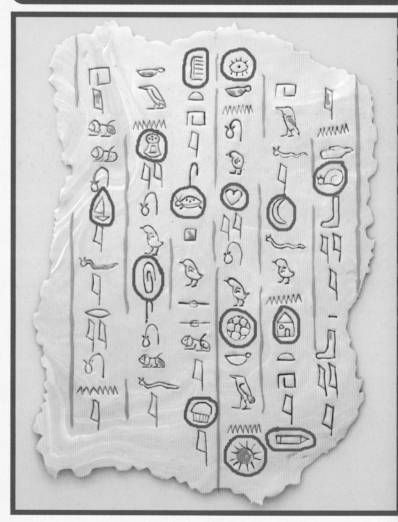

SEW IT UP

BUTTON HUNT

CRAYON CRAZE

BREAKFAST SPECIAL

DAYCARE EGGS

PARLOR GUESTS

BACKPACK BLAST

BALLOON FESTIVAL

FALLING LEAVES

NEEDLES IN A HAYSTACK